baby
Carla Harryman

Adventures in Poetry

The author wishes to thank the editors of *Crayon 3*, *Sal Mimeo 3* and *4*, *thedetroiter.com*, and *The Best American Poetry of 2004*.

Original cover art by Asa Watten
Book design by *typeslowly*
Printed in Michigan by Cushing-Malloy

Adventures in Poetry titles are distributed to the trade through Zephyr Press by Consortium Book Sales and Distribution [www.cbsd.com] and by SPD [www.spdbooks.org].

ISBN 0-9761612-1-4

9 8 7 6 5 4 3 2 FIRST PRINTING IN 2005

ADVENTURES IN POETRY
NEW YORK   BOSTON
WWW.ADVENTURESINPOETRY.COM

to. That. baby. Threshold.

To that. Baby. threshold.

Now. Word. Technology.

These were words she would learn someday. In the meantime she was fire in the womb with a skirt. Then a shirt which she pulled up through a small door that people on the other side called a cervical opening. Oh hallowed name and jittery shirt. She listened to a tiger reading files. She wanted to know what a tiger looks like, first. Before she wanted to know what anything else looked like. Someone, had that someone known anything about what baby wanted, would have said authoritatively it's the sound of the parent's voice you anticipate desire and suck in all at once through those perfect mitten ears and translucent and batted at things pulled red then formed into conch spindles then later shielded by hands from undesirable noise. The tiger opened a file claiming, this is the beginning of a long story. Which is everything baby wanted except the shirt she rolled up and over and in and by with for her skirt. The corner of everything was smitten with attentiveness. The difference between a womb and a room lies in such corners of attentiveness. Or the technology of listening.

Then. Apostrophe. Curve.

Sheaves of paper made from non-tree pulp but some new ecologically remunerative fiber rained on the floor so many it was like a waterfall and the tiger kept reading the story from them as they dropped. Willowy clamorous sounds in roaring nights those adjectives kept the tiger's voice thick with stalled thought. The tiger was not an impatient reader but her paws took unkindly to text. Some sheaves pierced through the claws, which would dart out when words such as such and entombment and liver and out fell out of her slobbering lips. This was an embarrassment, almost worse than incontinence, in the tiger universe, which prided itself in controlling the claws' revolt. The claws would have perfect timing. This was the first spiritual law of the tiger.

The story was about the possessive. To embrace for a very long time until the other finds her place in your fur. Purr. Purr. Baby can you hear me? Baby had fallen asleep. Against the curve of her mother's spine. Thus the tiger was able to hide her indignity and continue with her long recitation. How much, one might ask, did baby still know of this primordial shame, when years later and into adulthood she challenged the first spiritual law, the one

Tiger ≠ mother

Baby'' female

8

that admonished the tiger to hide and control her claws?
Baby had asked aloud, if the claw has a spontaneous life of
its own how are we to understand its nature if it must be
subject to one unyielding law? You are well on your way
to anarchy was the answer, which came from the world
of things. Humiliated, she hung her head and beheld her
arched feet and long toes upright in a universe of things.
Mostly the things were still indistinct, whirred surfaced
and bright but an old rattle, blue as a cucumber, held out
its hand and baby foraged in the hand's mitt and nestled
there for what seemed like another hundred years or so.

Spindle. Or. Cradle.

Green blades hanging in curves around a center bounce against lips squashed with dirt and a flaring nose dipping in close to one steady stalk. A spindle right up and sweetly still while blades all around cut air. Up top deep blue flower wings almost black at the tip and an ephemeral stripe where flower words lurk as it unfolds, singular and twinned on one stalk only. The others having been squirrel bitten off long before baby could sit in a garden a couple weeks back or so.

A twinned Siberian iris on a spindly stalk is what she knew. Something larger, absent in her consciousness begins to grow.

Or.

The hand is an insect perched on pee. Forgetting forgetting forests. This matter swelling in glee.

The Beginning of a Long Story Titled How Baby
Invented Allegory by the Tiger.

A long time ago the primordial goo didn't have a name, there were fewer names for things than there are now. It did have a sound: gee. The "g" in gee is pronounced with a hard g. It never sounds like a j. If one were to pronounce the sound jee too often back then when the industrial parks, aqueducts, and tract houses were only zip codes swimming in the vascular systems of certain miniscule insects, eons of progress would be erased in an instant. Gee. Gee. Say it often enough and it'll put you to sleep. Sleep sleep. Sleep is a good thing. If you must, go to sleep now. Fine. We can begin where we left off tomorrow.

So. Baby. Dreamed.
She was sucking on red blocks while batting her mother's nipples.

showing phonetic pronounciation of word

Dark. Swat. Land. *DARK*

Flung into the tunnel of love, baby was nervous when anything bounced. Shirt, skirt, pie, belly. Mangled and trounced binoculars. This and that this. And that. Windows. And a window pulled toward the door with mighty arms sinking beneath the floor. Alice gravely hic-cupping. Then sitting sitting and sitting. Sitting. For the four corners of the room subsided in the enormous hole. Movement was fear, a tiger, some kind of apple grinder breaking up asphalt. Caved in coughing. Land egg. Baby dream. Frothing. And E go. Certain sounds rigid formu-las thought. Attract futures stuck in happy land. Give me liberty or give me death had not history in baby's breath. But sound of force struck in her trunk. Here and then beginning of baby's not. And not.

unspoken

Baby.
Baby was a modernist. What is the feeling of freedom?

tiger = Baby's Fear

Clout. Hide. Mirror.

And so the tiger's story continued with a complex explanation of primordial goo. It was not your typical mythic story about various atavistic gods in the form of animals and avatars seeming to take form from mud and mist. It was more like an analysis than a harkening of the auditor toward a beginning of time. The auditor, who we call the baby, enjoyed both sensations: the sensation of being led into the surrounding comfort of a story, cradled as she was in the voice of the storyteller heralding the disappearance of the material world, and the sensation of abstraction, which required she situate herself within another kind of mental labyrinth, one that engaged the effects of the material world toward objective systems of thought. She found what anybody could find, that after many repetitions of systems of narration and systems of objectification the distinctions between them became blurred. As the separation between object and narration became less and less obvious, webs of knowledge systems replaced stable concepts. These systems took hold in the mind, which reproduced them in variations that indicated an infinity under construction.

Clout?

Hide

Mirror

Thesis

Twins: Story + Abstraction

Everything comes with instructions

The two black maples baby examined every morning showed her something about a particular mental capacity. They were perfectly lined up, such as to resemble twins. As twins, they entered a potential story full of ribs and veins and possibly attacking vines held at bay by martyred gardeners in sun hats and the twining musculature of jungle avatars in comic books. But even when they were observed from the upper story window, as they so often were, and perceptually cut into sections by the schematic lines of the window, baby noticed that in her mind she was able to create an idea of the trees as a twinned, a mirrored unity, uninterrupted by narrow framing, but organized by a pre-inclination toward seeing things in pairs, symmetrically such that she could mentally erase even the huge limbs of the ash tree that draped itself over the perceptual field of the black maples. Since the tiger understood all of these things about baby's mental activities, she knew that her story about the genesis of primordial good, the derivative of goo, would need to be complex.

Toward. Some. Air.

It was another representation baby hadn't represented. Hadn't known to represent. A fellow feeling swallowed down into her stomach, her gut bulged and her hands looked for someplace to go. She was behind bars yelling at injustice and ignored again.

Here the bookshelves were numerous, high to distraction and up she saw to the top. Look. Look. A bunny was high up on one of them, unscrewing a light bulb. Hah. The lights are going to go out and there will be in the dark a baby, bunny, shelves of books, and a prison from which to scream again and again. That's silent night. Deep black holes surrounding warm-blooded creatures yelling. Bunny lost her footing and bounced onto a desk, up into the air, and down onto baby who didn't at all like the fur on her tongue and spit a lot but quietly while the bunny struggled for her life until she didn't know what was going to happen. The bunny froze behind a pillow except for the autonomous nose that fascinated baby who thought it was a bee.

Help. Bunny.

And so we return to the tiger's allegory. For literature is that which operates on the premise that objects including parents, babies, and bunnies are conduits to vast conceptual machines.

The baby listened with her mouth puckered in dirt, her shirt tied to her knees, her mellow skirt full of bees up around her neck and her blue jeans dangling from the clothesline under the claws of an old crow. She had been building a hole in the dirt out next to the rose bushes. Something or someone said don't go near the rose bushes. So she had stopped just short of that. Someone or something over there was watching. She threw her shovel into the hole and sat on the edge of it with her feet dangling down into it. The tiger looked at her and said, you are right, usually there's someone watching. Baby thought that was fine.

You are getting older said the tiger. You are wandering in a woods thinking about eating berries. You realize that you aren't hungry but you want the berries anyway. You come to the edge of the woods and out beyond them is a large lake. You tell the old crow sitting up there on the clothes-

line that out there between the shore and the horizon is
a blueberry shrub. You don't know why you tell the crow
this thing. The lake is perfect without anything in it. But
you keep looking for something to put in it. You love how
peaceful it seems, yet you want to see somebody swim by.
The crow flies away and now you are all alone. Why did
the crow fly away? you ask yourself. Then you ask yourself
why must there be a berry bush in the middle of the lake?
And why a swimmer? If you swim for a long time, you
will be hungry for the berries. You will look for the ber-
ries halfway between the shore and the horizon. You want
someone else to do this. You like people to bring things
to you, but you can tell that no one will help you. I am a
tiger and I am telling you this now. No one will help you.
Someone far away is wondering about you, but they can't
read your thoughts which are now propelling you toward
the water. You take off your clothes and when you touch
the water it swallows you like a big mouth. But the mouth
spits you out and you are flying. You fall on the berry bush.
It scratches you up but you float on it for a long time. You
look back at the shore and the woods are very small. You
feel like sleeping and you feel a dream coming on and you
try to stop the dream. You think you are successful. There
are no berries on the bush and the shore is a long way off.

knowledge? (handwritten margin note)

lesson? (handwritten margin note)

This is not dreaming you say to yourself. This is called being alone. Then you try to decide if you were more alone when you were in the woods before you had put the berry bush in the lake. This is all my doing you say to yourself. When I was on land I was watched and now no one can see me. With these words a berry appears fully ripe on the bush. If I eat this berry I will be alone again. It is blue, gleaming, plump. The wind tugs at the branches. It is certainly going to fall off. Baby, what are you going to do?

Baby looked at the tiger who seemed a little tangled up and cockeyed. A ball of string dangled from its mouth. How did that get there? asked baby. She began to tug at the string. The string uncoiled easily. After baby had wrapped each plant in the garden, including the roses, with string, connecting them all to each other, she found herself back at the hole with the tiger who still held the end of the string in her mouth.

In. Interim. Term.

For the heavy life and soaking fears are remedies gliding with ferocious gestures. Toes jammed into a book, the only one in that house, and crumpled now.

Baby. In Many Houses.

Lounge lizard. Stealth. Quiet music. Gap and gappy mouth. With feeling and again with feeling. Above the bench. They are feeling. The keys to the piano. Bark a little. And cranky. With manicotti. Again.

And. An Interval with Teenagers.

Baby knew that someday she would be a child and then a teenager and then an adult and that child, teenager, and adult would never be able to live without her. She would always be part of them. And each one now also had a baby in him or her. Babies lived longer than anybody, for anytime a child could no longer bear the burden of childhood, she or he could regress to that prior condition called babyhood. Baby also knew, because she spent a lot of time with adults, more time than did children or teenagers, that regression was a word that gave babies a bad rap. Her strategy however was to use the word in a positive light rather than to be offended by it. Baby was always hard to offend unless someone took something away from her. The kind of being least likely to take anything away from her was a teenager. Unlike children, teenagers knew better than to imitate adults. They were quite specifically rational creatures. Teenagers watched, listened, waited, were subtle and not quick to judge. They also minded their own business and rather optimistically expected the rest of the world to reciprocate. Few people, other than teenagers themselves, were ever capable of such reciprocity. Even baby, whose vast admiration for the teenager as a species was nearly infinite, could not help but riddle the teenager,

How teens look to baby

How baby sees teens from seeing her.

upon occasion, with a barrage of laughter or stand on or in the teenager's shoes if the teenager wasn't wearing them. It was difficult to stand in both of them at one time and her effort to stay upright in each shoe only served to increase baby's admiration for the teenager. The teenager seemed to tolerate baby's antics, was sometimes even delighted by them. The teenager's delight surprised baby. This gave baby pause. Surprise is *my* job thought baby. But baby was in love and didn't complain when the teenager took the surprise away from her. In fact, this is how baby learned that there was an endless supply of surprise to go around and, that in this knowledge, she was more like a teenager than either a child or adult. One day it occurred to her that the teenager was also like *her*. On this day, baby swelled with pride. No one knew why baby had had such a good day, why she had babbled to herself, why she had not socked at and chewed dust mites and pieces of thread lodged in the rug or tried to nurse the pink balloon lost under a bed for about six hours. Or pulled all of the utensils off the table while tugging at the tablecloth. She was peaceful, quiet and perfect for an entire day. Baby knew that when children threw tantrums and acted grabby they were "behaving like babies." Adults acted like children acting like babies quite frequently themselves.

For children, when they whined and argued, used the strategies they had learned from adults. The impassioned use of logic, argumentation, and judgment were all signs that they were about to cry, shriek, rail, and sulk. Their beloved rationality was the beveled awning of a madhouse. All of them had a baby part hidden inside of them ready to wreak havoc on home and country. But the teenager, in all his and her wisdom, emulated only those qualities in baby others considered charming. Teenagers surely used their sang-froid as a kind of magic, to keep the infantile child and adult world out of their hair. It was baby whom teenagers permitted to play in that hair. Baby therefore knew that teenagers were the best, the most mature creatures on earth. Adults were often irked by the teenager's silence, and sometimes called it sullen. But baby knew the silence was a product of an unaffected poise. Teenagers were sage beyond their years because they loved to surprise and to be surprised, but to surprise anybody in this vexed and over-anxious world of consumer culture and professional parenting, one had to act as if one were in a steady state or holding pattern most of the time. Maintaining this mask in the face of everybody and everything else required great powers. Teenagers ought to be put in greater positions of responsibility claimed baby and to be given the vote by thirteen, or fourteen at the very latest.

Baby. In Three Parts.

Baby has discovered a kind of no name narcissism not because she knows the meaning of narcissism and wants to convert self-adoration into something invisible, filthy, eager, peppery with sweat, and universally altruistic. Not because she even means to love herself. Intention switches places with the disquisition of lungs bursting with her smarts withering future word balloons.

Next baby is in hiding. She is going to praise something not worth knowing. No worth. No verdict. Salty lips wrangle with mist. Clotted clouds devour a sky. The goodness of good words of Kantian aesthetics blow amongst flimsy detail for the round world amplifies a life of its own, a life on its own, an anti-aesthetic with revolt, a wish list or one and one and one steeped in spikes, fingers, and holes. She the gargantuan fragment pulls on the thin lower branch of an oak tree then pulverizes one and then another oak leaf. With these new forms of flesh jammed into each of her fists she marches into daddy's room, mounts his seated lap, and smothers his forehead with the application of leaves. Her father in this play begins his history of fretting for his little girl, whom he predicts is destined to the life of the artist. Baby willfully disregards the codes-tossed-in-

fret, but as an afterthought, she presents her father with an alternative code: this is for nothing, for no one, for it and me. Come here daddy and look into the glands of a fearless flower.

"All thinking hears the indelible imprint of survival." Once upon a time baby wallowed in trivia so that no one could associate her wallowing with shame. Baby figured that if she could live in this inchoate world where her actions were neither confirmed nor denied, some great force would bubble up around her and we'd all turn into ferocious beasts. Her body would dissolve into the Realm of Ferocity and she would live shamelessly ever after.

Next.

Small mean feats and regurgitation of memories made baby wild. She melted into the crowd. I frantically followed her certain all the while she would meet her doom before the fatal hour when moths let loose a scent that compels humanity to respire most willfully. Creatures fallen from grace including show horses and several unfortunate mud hens pranced and scuttled unwittingly through the compositional nightmare. Did baby know where she was going? Absurdity after absurdity stunted my search for baby. The moths swooped around a slanted tree. A derailed train lightly nudged its trunk, which was torn away slightly from its surface roots. Bankers, stockbrokers, and sales people of all stripes marched up and down the sidewalks as invisibly as if they were in Midtown Manhattan.

The sun was lowering slowly and I was frantic to find baby. If I were to call on a cop for assistance I would be asked for my credentials. These credentials, neatly tucked into my sock, were wilting with sweat. The stench would prove that I was a lazy even abusive parent.

I thought I heard baby at a distance. When one loses baby, the body comes nearly undone. Your guts start to strangle your organs and your limbs take flight. Suddenly I recognized the location: San Francisco. This was good. I knew this town.

At nightfall, I thought I saw baby standing on a soapbox made of musical instrument cases stacked precariously one on top of the other. At an artificial height of four and one half feet she was a commanding young figure. Like gaudy acrobats, her dimpled arms flung up over her head every time she wanted the crowd surrounding her to cheer or egg her on. There she was, or so it seemed, exercising her rights to free speech again. As I approached, my view of baby was obliterated by onlookers. When I could see again, the musicians were unpacking the instruments from the cases: the soapbox had been dismantled. The musicians tuned their strings, sucked on mouthpieces, then began to play a sad tune:

> Hold me
> Hold on
> Waiting for curfew
> To go home

It's night
Bright lights
Fling fear
Away

Hold on
It's night
Bright lights
Fling fear away

Let's play
A tune
Waiting for curfew
To go home

I left before it was over. And yet, it didn't seem to matter
at all if I stayed or went. Baby would be raped and mur-
dered by now kidnapped or placed in a holding cell at the
police station or given to a foster family or placed under
observation in a social worker's clinic. Or she would be
hiding in the basement with some local cur and her pups,
feeding with the pups from the cur's nipples and drinking
out of the same water dishes. Someplace out there was the
real, the reality principle, even reality and realism all tied

up in a bundle waiting for the flood of investors to snatch the whole thing up. That's where baby could be found. But "I" I was left here in the imagination, strangling in the pearls before swine she'd smothered me with, intoxicated by the false scent wafting around the urban rot of baby's noisy dreams.

Again. The. Time.
Repetition and baby. Losing and tiger baby. Water in baby
and curling. Ears and accumulation. To know everything.
Baby is entirely inside baby. Then baby glides, a little boat,
and not interruption. She doesn't want an imposition. She
seals tiger's mouth with her wet tongue. This is tiger silent.
A hand dances with a knee. Silently things have fallen
around baby. The sun taking a bath, says baby.

no more fear

Yelling. For. Fun.
Someone produces frequent groans. Flowers ornament
the walls. Out is getting out and being out. And being out
getting out.

Theory. Of. Prose ◯ —no. period. ↳ why?

Recuperate. Her. Loss.

Features. Distinguish. Between.

Beginning. At. End.

Over. At. Barn.

Nonexistent. Twin. Sick.

I. Am. Well.

Whiteness. Is. Cruel.

Act. That. Out.

Just. To. Be.

Better. Than. Poor.

Act. Out. Poor.

Better. Be. Poor.

As. White. Dust.

30

Mutations.
In the air cuddling with the wildest regions. Reproducing one trauma after another. This is it. Baby's life was getting longer. It was becoming historical.

Mutations.
A face with red cavernous gashes and things possibly living in them. Possibly pill bugs, dragonflies, freedom fighters, and tiny horses. Then eyes as large and black as truck tires but with irises and pupils as gentle and wary as a handsome mammal's. Exaggeration is better than bricks and squares. Baby's ancestors knew this and baby is holding the hands of her ancestors. They all reject banality and drink from the lake with their necks curved in arches. Someday baby will declare that people are horses locked in upright bodies. That most of western architecture is a product of repression. This is why she cannot, will not ever wear shoes.

The. Corner. Of.
The whole lot is now dark and out of sorts. The corner then finally vanishes. Lashed. Lacerated. Then the pain is gone. Something too hot to even sting exits the tongue along with everything.

White clothes. Diminutive.
white. is over skin. shrinking it a little. all other colors be-
long. belong to me. (don't tell). if for the skin. to the eyes.
accented. spies. possessive ones. dressed me up. that's why
dirt. encourages. hems. hems mollify. earth tones. touch
the ground. in humility. abandon. (don't tell). my disguised
humility. "abandon (don't tell)." the white clothes whisper.

(Voice).
the white clothes also whisper. to be measured and sub-
stantiated. from being the antagonist. or devourer of
space. the voice begins to be our accomplice.

Therefore. Get it.
get a good recording.

Artifact.

But the tiger teaches. Tiger teaches. → fear teaches?

Once, said the tiger, the forest was angry. What forest? asked baby. I'll tell you soon. Hang on. Once the forest was angry and thought balloons melted inside it. What were balloons doing in the forest? I'll tell you in a minute. One of the thought balloons had said, the water is getting too close. When the thought balloon melted because a forest's anger can sometimes melt a thought balloon, the water in the balloon's thoughts surrounded the trees. Why didn't the water sink into the ground? The ground was already wet, very wet. The ground was so wet that the water couldn't sink quickly. The trees were angry and now they were getting sick. Where did they hurt? Trees feel everything all over. They get mad and drop their leaves. Some of them began to drop their leaves. Where was the forest? The forest was way up north. Use your finger and point that way. The baby was standing up in her crib, which she had more or less outgrown but liked to be in it now that she knew how to get out.

A reaching padded paw surrounded then covered baby's pudgy fist, which seemed as putty for the paw. Claws as silky as ivory sweaters unfurled from the paw. These claws formed delicate pincers around baby's index finger, then pulled carefully, uncurling the finger out from under her plump fist. As if they were showing the finger the key to the future, the claws directed it toward the window with the view of oak trees. That's north. Something insurmountable woke baby from her sensual trance. She grabbed her own index finger with her opposite thumb, making of her thumb a vice for the finger. She proceeded to study the finger as meticulously as would a tiger, rotating it in its socket and bending it back a little and then out. She then retracted her hand, holding it in close to her chest. Then the hand thrust outward with the index finger rigid as a pole pointing north. That way is north. So north was now in her body, forever.

The. Open. Box.

Baby in another era was running from room to room with her arm thrust out and her finger bent in a peculiar position. She was making a splattering buzzing sound. A black fly in the form of baby! That ran splat right into the television set perched on a little stool. A stool baby had used only yesterday. Wha's 'at? asked baby, pointing at the TV screen. The tiger was there ready to whisper in her ear. It's a dungeon full of dirt. Oh, zee, zee, said baby in wonderment pulling at the knobs. Tiger realized too late baby liked dungeons full of dirt, especially when description poured spontaneously out of tiger's mouth. Baby loved the mouth of the tiger. Especially its sweaty lips. So the TV, it was black and white, went pop, on. Baby sat down on the floor with her entire hand in her mouth, her mouth sucking on the hand, four and five fingers. In and out. While nutty adults in miniature did all sorts of things talking in odd theatrical voices as if they were talking to air and air could listen. The air has huge ears, thought baby. She looked around all about her but could only feel the air brushing lightly against her cheeks in that interstitial world between now and then. In the meantime, the jackpot hobnobbing of the nitwits and sad sacks on television had vanished. In front of her was an emaciated child with huge ribs and a terrible listless look that frowned on baby's chubby face. Baby fearlessly batted at the TV screen. The baby's in the box. The baby's in the box! The baby's in the box! The box! Open the box now!

Entombment. Liver. Such.

Baby's drawing was a monument as large as the mountains. On the outside of the tomb, or the mountains, a colossal collaboration between people and nature was underway. People built roads and easy access waterfall paths and came in droves to see the beautiful sites, to fish, perhaps to hunt nearby, and to grow more fish also. Somewhere at a distance on other government controlled lands, the trees were cut down in multitudes, animals lost their homes and died. The mountains retaliated with horrible floods washing down the bald sides of hills killing everything in the way, since nature did not make a distinction between any living or non living thing and any other living or non living thing. This version of nature was the opposite of all the ciphers baby had learned to date. Baby wondered how in her drawing she would label the undecipherable parts of this world. There were areas such as "walkways," "paths," "roads," "falls," "rocky domes," "camping," "nature preserve." There was also a vast uncertainty that no caption suited. Not "ripped to shreds angry mountainous regions," not "dangerous wilderness area," or "havoc," or "keep out," or "the rest is silence."

Baby needed to enter the tomb and she needed a way to mark things without destroying the disorganized face of nature. Deciding to combine the two projects, as they seemed mysteriously related, baby journeyed to the edge of the unnamable aspect of the world where she cut open her body to expose her liver to the birds. A bird came and ate a piece of her liver then swooped into a cave. Baby entered the cave also, following the sound of the bird's wings to a place with a lot of bats. There she thought she could see in the dim light an owl eating a bat. She wondered if the owl had been the bird that had led her there. As she was thinking this thought, the bats began to laugh; apparently they could read her mind. Self consciously, she looked down at her naked body: her liver had been covered over with a scar. She was now marked with experience and this gave her a feeling of great depth, which was appropriate anyway since she was now ensconced within the depths of the vast cave, or tomb, or mountains.

Just as on the outside of the mountains there were only certain places she could go, so here on the inside there was an edge between where she could and could not travel. She wondered if she could stay on this border. If she lost her bearings she would drown, be smothered in mud, be consumed by a wildfire, trampled, eaten by wild creatures, or starve. Baby wondered if there was a caste system in the tomb. Did those who receive official burial, and adventurers who had met their death by accident, and those who had been tossed into it violently ever communicate with each other as spirits? Was there a hierarchy of the dead? Baby was wondering all of this as she was padding in her tough little feet alongside a labyrinth, half looking for its outer exit and half enjoying the feeling of her hand on her round belly, which somehow seemed to nourish her thinking process.

She was therefore greatly surprised when a teenager swaggered through an opening in the labyrinth, stood right in front of baby, and began speaking the unspeakable. The teenager told baby that she and her friends had been listening to her weird thoughts for a couple of hours and they recommended she just keep going on her way, back toward the exit. You are about to enter the adult prison. Baby, who loved teenagers more than anything in the world, was ready with savvy words of protest. Hey, said baby, how ya doin'. But the teenager wouldn't take the lure. You wanna die or somethin'? But who would want to kill baby? Look, I'm okay, said baby. You're a baby! Baby had never heard before the derogatory undertone of her erstwhile glorious label. This is my drawing and I can go where I want, are the thoughts that baby did not express, but you can't talk that way to a teenager and she knew it; instead, baby asked the teenager what she was doing in an adult prison. Well, I ate some bullshit for breakfast and they locked me up 'cause they found some of it left on my person. Now I'm becoming a killer. The teenager threw a rock into the abyss. That's either me, or you.

Such was the law of the entombed teenager. Laws tend to create the urges for speechmaking in certain precocious creatures, so baby speechified to herself all the way out of the cave, distracted and disembodied and somehow led to the surface of the world by instinct, since she was not paying attention to where she was going. Something hard in her was driving her, producing words, slogans, and arguments against such forms of criminalization as she had witnessed. For her life had become, as if by magic the threat of annihilation of another, the teenager, to whom she felt indebted forever. To baby, teenager first meant joy. When she reached the surface of the world and faced again the horrific site of the spoiled mountains, she defiled the hitherto unnamable part of the mountain with words from a revelation. With big clumsy baby letters she wrote out the words State Death then sat back on her haunches looking down at her map in grief stricken astonishment as if she were peering into the shroud of her own best impulses.

Another Artifact.

Open lips for sucking and pouting were all stopped up with a plug that wouldn't come out. Without result, lips and teeth tugged on the plug of a wasp-waisted object. Baby's hands were moist as usual so she wiped them down the side of her shirt. But she couldn't pull the stopper out even with the use of her wadded up shirt, which she had finally struggled out of. A voice from behind her said, it isn't supposed to open. Hands pried baby's digits away dislodging the object, which was returned then to a shelf and set between a portrait of baby and a kachina doll with green pants and something earnest about it moving forward. For a minute baby looked around for her shirt. It had apparently disappeared along with the door shutting. Baby's lips moved in and out in a sucking pout as she contemplated the wasp-waisted relic on the shelf. The object was obviously the physical manifestation of the inside of a song bound up methodically around the middle with twine. Such fortification caused baby to place her hand two inches below her navel and rub there with a circular motion. Her belly was getting hot and her body was tuning up. Eee sounds rose clear and up into her throat from her navel. If there had been silence, silence would have been pierced but the room was always humming.

Knowledge. *turn*

Knowledge was being processed. It was in the argument machine and the driver of the machine was a god with the face of a man and the body of an inkbottle.

Knowledge.

White fuzz in the air froze on a screen. Baby danced the cancan which she'd seen imitations of on daytime television. Monarch butterflies hatched that day blanketing the scruffy shrubs with anxiety. Baby danced on the sidewalk. She choked a coke can with a jump rope. Then blew up a plane with her semi-automatic spitballs. The butterflies wanted nothing to do with her. When she trapped them with her little hands, they played dead, and when she opened her hands, they wobbled on air pockets off into trees. These children, these children, screamed baby. What do they know?

(War Cycle)

Baby's War.
Someone asked baby what she thought about the war.
Baby went to her closet and threw on some clothes. Other
clothes were all over.

Baby invited the interviewer into her room. She invited
the stranger to try on the clothes on the floor. Some of
them baby had worn just twice and some of them a hun-
dred or so times.

War Times.
They were far from here and they were here. They were
far and falling mistakes. Of times and timing. Time was
far from here. Here was just here. Something happening
in a book. This is it. This is now. The book. The window. A
pencil x-ing out images of furrows in earth, land mines in
the desert, and mangling. These mangled things x-ed are
far and now and once upon a time. The past was here in a
book and after the book had been destroyed it was as if the
war were over in the felt land where what was seen pierced
and the window closed and the window closed.

Baby. N. Baseball. Song.

Baby was going to sing and then sing twice. The song was later attenuated when there was nothing left to bring to the foreground of the forest, which had been the center of singing as baby experienced her lungs. Experience. Experience. She sang. She sang divided and then twice feeling the lungs of the forest as her own and then stepping back to observe herself as such phenomenon springing into readymade denomination from the head of an old god named Nietzsche. Or N. His name too had been clipped short like the song when she, growing tired and distracted, had less and less to bring forth as offering, as person, to the forest, which was transforming into high speed blur. Tings like notes left distinct prints in non-voiced ground near voiced air. These were things baby could not experience or express. She recuperated her energies and opened her mouth. She thought she was going to taste tings. Then she thought again and thus was thinking twice. The singing was attenuated, clipped short. Minor distractions delineated something back in the brain that her lips associated with sucking.

Baby's little body is a speedball. That's what someone re-marked as she raced back and forth between the catcher's mound and home plate. Someone was watching her play. She is her own ball. This someone was laughing so baby flew into sky and ground.

Note.

There they were. The notes clipped. Short, spread out. Deathless and. Without design. Baby was trying to decide if she should let go the cry pressing up through her chest when the sound of children distracted her. Were they surrounding her? The children are coming. The children are coming. She sang. Wailed. Rolled into a speedball and proceeded on her back and forth diagonal course from h. plate to p. mound. Baby was not a team player. The shifting universe had narrowed to one demand: do not give up the strip of inside field. Singing, wailing, were trampled in the dust of a play that cut all others out.

Baby. (For B and T)

Because this is the literature of ideas I cannot smoke a cigar. Baby had picked it up in the parking lot at the market.

Because this is the literature of ideas what just happened is a thought. Baby would give the cigar to Uncle Ted. Uncle Ted liked a musician named Sun Ra. He was from outer space.

When baby's father inquired as to where the cigar had come from, the one that baby had wedged on the tight ledge between head and ear, baby had the answer. This cigar is from outer space. It was a surprise for Ted from Sun Ra.

(Suburb Cycle)

Baby's [M]other. Picture. Perfect. Song.
Heard her mother say, I feel that I should do something.
I feel like I should get out more I feel I could use some
adult company I feel I've forgotten how to think.
     I feel.
     I feel.
Sang baby. I feel I feel I feel I feel I feel I feel I feel.
She was setting these words to row row row your boat
while pinching a piece of dust that had been trapped be-
tween her toes in the otherwise spotless house.

An. Other. Baby.
That baby is a spoiled brat. That baby is spoiled spoiled
spoiled. That baby sacrifices to a willful design ignoring ev-
erything everything. That baby makes up projects — some
huge appendage is added to the house in the hot sun — and
almost dies from heat, sweetly, like a forest turned inside
out, and slowly while others nurse that baby back to health
to waking life to scam and wham "I am a man" with stature
humming in a car.

Tragedy.
That baby loved a cop show. That baby thrives on no no.
That baby. That baby.

Tragedy. Reconsidered.

You've gotta throw yourself at the other baby because you've been abandoned and forsaken. The other baby ridicules and ridicules. And you are left left left there. Left and thrown down and the other baby gets under you and licks the wounds that gird the fine figure you cut when you are hiding the truth: you are just a baby. The other baby who has ridiculed and tormented you and who now soothes you with tongue and a special silence, abandons you, goes to work, mercilessly. And you baby of babies stand out, among the wild albatross, shining and shining "when the sun goes down."

Go. Down. Sun.
Be with baby under baby.

On. Silence. (for Alan Davies)
why touch cap
baby stirs wilderness
owns nothing
spice and spice
her wavelets
wavelets own
their own
baby
and baby possession
of baby
cap
in hate hat
it stinks hat
time it and
stink own
a way
through the spring
caps
wavelets booing
shoot bamboo
a bit of torture
now

In. My. Sin.

Baby heard the singer singing in my sin. Sin was a good word, fun to say and say wrong for sin and thin were close. Very close. Sin was halfway between thin and fin. Baby's friend Finn was sailing with the sharks but baby knew the difference between fin and Finnian, the formal name of Finn. Although sin sounded close to fin and thin, it was abstract. Baby didn't know the meaning of sin, except as a sound associated with other sounds, sounds that meant things. Abstraction caused baby to babble in my thin fin in my fin sin Finnian's in thin fin's sin. Sin was nonsense, a kind of nonsense associated with things that made meaning. And so being in one's sin was being in everything and everything was the same as being in the world. Baby was in the world and knew it through sin, or singing.

One day baby was seated in the pebbled courtyard of the abbey under hot sun singing and singing. Organ music flew out of the abbey's chapel and hit the wall of heat that separated everything way up into shreds of clouds from baby's singing. It was strong singing and hot as a furnace, which may have been why some monks and tourists and souvenir sales people were scowling at baby's song, an improvised song inspired by organ music. Drunk with song mingling with organ music, baby was oblivious to formality. Like nonsense, the song united with everything. The song *was* nonsense, a nonsense as sound as stern people's judgments of her budding character.

Wartime. Surroundings.

There were the surroundings baby had nibbled at. And the plum jam spilled on the surroundings. There were some larded bits of a piecrust baked for her quick while the giant pie for everybody baked and baked. Baby had heard the word nerve gas and thought that the kitchen smells were nerve gas. They made your nerves stand alert. Baby was running on the fuel of love, skidding to a halt at the kitchen door, then plunging back into the railthin kitchen with gusto until she reached some destination, which was erratically determined by the magnitude of her own physical force. The giant pie for everybody in the meantime was taking a long time to cook. What if it doesn't come out? she wanted to know. What if something is in there wrecking it? The anticipation was getting on her nerves. She wanted it to come out now. She had her plans, she was going to give that pie to the fat cats. She'd heard talking about those fat cats — out somewhere high rolling. Baby loved animals and wanted to feed the high rolling fat cats. She told the tiger she wanted to watch the fat cats eat pie and why didn't it hurry up. If you don't watch out, you'll be running for president. I hope the fat cats like pie, said baby. The tiger bit her lip and a tear rolled down her cheek, you're gonna break my heart. Well, you can have pie too — baby felt magnanimously toward tiger, who was as precise with a fork as she was spontaneous with a bag of sugar. What if I told you I was hoping to feed the pie to something scrawny and wild? asked tiger. There aren't any fat cats around here and that nerve gas, well, isn't really nerve gas. What you smell is a drop of fear sweetened by pie.

Smell. Of. Pie.
When baby grew up, the smell of pie would sometimes knock her out.

More. Surroundings.

Baby moved from household to household. She was a universal figure. She cut a pretty picture. There she was in some kind of upstairs domain and then she was low to the ground. Dirt was coming up through the floor. Somebody was always washing her hands. She heard someone mention the hands of providence one day, and this scared her. She hid her hands inside her pants and under her skirt, behind her back, and in some secret deep pockets where she kept a lot of fluff tantamount to the sum total of insignificant pleasantries exchanged among strangers all over the earth on any given day. She feared someone was going to take her hands away.

National. Identity. Question.

Baby began to speculate. If my hands are mine. They are mine. My hands. One of them wandered into her mouth. A finger wiggled a tooth loose at the roots, a palm slushed around on the tongue, the rough of her mouth was a dome of the cave that led one to the entrance of the impassable jungle. A sandy scent surprised her: it seemed to be welling up into her nostrils from someplace out of reach. Where did this come from? She pulled out and searched the primordial hand as if it were a slimy traitor. What were you doing in my mouth?

Reeling.

Reeling backward, then again, until her windmill arms flung to the floor. Forced to the floor baby sees her future lying there. Baby observer of body, observes body, and serves gravity with her body. Acting out a drama and yelling, fall to the earth fall to the earth, hit the dirt. Whirling upward then sinking she follows her own directions downward. Collapsed and downward bruised within an exhilarated aching. She defies pain with accelerated force dancing out of control. Pain isn't hurting she cries when nobody's listening.

Integrity.

She heard it. A big N crashing in on her preoccupations. That line has no N tegrity. No N. Then everything else was a blur. The language had force and baby's thoughts ran.

Shapes.

Words had power, compelling force. Shapes made the throat open.

Baby. And Be. (for Erik Mortenson)

Baby wanted to be just where she was, the way a fly swat-
ter is exactly where it is at the moment of contact with a
fly. You are a little Buddha. A parent or someone, baby re-
ally hadn't been paying much attention, was attempting to
smother a concept with words. So baby agreed with them.
Oh, yes, I know just what you mean. Well, that silenced
them, and little fly swatters made contact with flies in the
four squares of the sunroom.

Cruelty.

Cruelty is the worst. With her right hand, baby was bend-
ing the fingers of her left hand backward one at a time up
to the point she thought something would hurt. Cruelty.
The fly swatter was on the floor at her side, a performing
object or supplicant. It doesn't matter who you are, she
patted the fly swatter, I should not have abused you in that
manner! You can't help it if you were made to kill, but I
didn't have to facilitate your murders.

Oh. Cruelty.

Unseemly uncles with pushcarts and grandfathers multiplied. Leaves of the trees turned on the branches, loosening, loosening. They were going to shake brown while storming generalities swilled in her curls. Then there were the wild aunts gathering around running water with their carving knives while trampled clothes lay face down and knotted in the elsewhere of the caged soul. Dotted fabric smothered a lacy scarf. Cousins locked the door behind them. There was no escape and an overabundance of laughter.

Force.

The door opens. Oh.

Come. In.

Aack. That command. A demand from Europe or Vishnu. It's best to misunderstand or swear that nothing happened. No leaves in the yard. No yard. No wax. No wick. No sugar. No sugar daddy. And onward. Or *in* just plain in without onward. No magnet drew the body toward it. There are so many children, so why does it matter what I do?

Sheer. Weather.

What can happen between a shotgun and head spot? Doorjamb and lily clot? Diseases. That she knew. Who was sick today? Why were they storming in and out taking her tiger away? Then she saw a high-strung family. The idea was too much. All of them, the family, the idea, forbidden clothespins stretched up beyond reach. And as potent as a tiny drop of blood on the sleeve of her shirt rubbing against the cut she had acquired from the far-flung behavior of the sewing shears.

Is there. Any.

An embrace presented itself before she had had the opportunity to reject it. How odd thought baby. Underneath relaxes in the hands of a trusted soul. Any hands might do. Is there a word for this phenomenon, she wondered or should I forget it now and move there where the flat stones lead me into the garden warming and even burning but only a little the bottom of my feet. Then there will be soft shade and perhaps a new tiger.

Doubling Cycle (for Amy Claire) *Actress*

Doubling.
Limbs sweat. Trees sweat. Baby sweats.

Doubling. Doubling.
Limbs sweat. Trees sweat. Kiss and float. Baby sweats. And floats. Design is everything. It can't help baby. And baby doesn't need help. Highway heat is manageable. Walk down the road and the cars are all ventriloquists. They want you to go home, but they've given their authority over to unified honking. Just keep walking and sweating. The trees are waiting and the cars can't climb like a baby.

When. Looking.

When looking back she saw a scar on the car hood in a dream. The dream had been a real dream and she was looking back at it, but it was not available for discussion. It was only a dream, no one else could see it or know it. The scar. The hood of the car combined with the scar. It was curious. This religion of skin for which there was no titular value.

The use of language in primordial ways. language as a primordial too

Tiger = Baby's After-ego Suggesthe Culture